Cosmic Grooves:

Cancer

by Jane Hodges

CHRONICLE BOOKS
SAN FRANCISCO

RHINO

Text copyright © 2001 Chronicle Books LLC
Executive Producer: Andrea Kinloch
Compilation Produced for Release: Dave Kapp, Mark Pinkus, and Andrea Kinloch
Remastering: Bob Fisher at Pacific Multimedia Corp.
Licensing: Wendi Cartwright
Project Assistance: Patrick Milligan, Amy Utstein, Mary Patton, and Mason Williams

Rhino Entertainment Company
10635 Santa Monica Blvd.
Los Angeles, California 90025
www.rhino.com

Library of Congress Cataloging-in-Publication Data available.

ISBN 0-8118-3059-4

Printed in China

Designed by Michael Mabry
Illustration copyright © 2001 Michael Mabry

Distributed in Canada by Raincoast Books
9050 Shaughnessy Street
Vancouver, British Columbia V6P 6E5

10 9 8 7 6 5 4 3 2 1

Chronicle Books LLC
85 Second Street
San Francisco, California 94105
www.chroniclebooks.com

Cancer
June 22 to July 22

Element: *Water*

Quality: *Cardinal, a sign that leads others*

Motto: *"I feel"*

Planetary Ruler: ☽ *The Moon, the planet of feelings and the unconscious*

Moon's Influence: *Cancerians are highly sensitive, empathetic people who instinctively respond to others' emotions. Like the phases of the Moon, their moods change often. These intuitive people are capable of great compassion and are often very artistic. However, the sensitivity that is their gift has a downside: They can also be very spiteful when hurt.*

Symbol: *Crab*

Crab's Influence: *Cancerians are gentle and emotional, but they will retreat into their shells if they feel attacked. While they make wonderfully nurturing parents and partners, on those rare instances when they choose to fight an enemy their pincers can hurt. Cancerians revere the past and history, and can hang on to memories. While they have trouble letting go of grudges, they also make sentimental, sweet friends.*

How to recognize a Cancer:
Wide eyes and face, delicate thin skin, affectionate hugger
Pick-up line: *"Tell me about your mother."*

What a Cancer wants:
Safe home, sensitivity
What a Cancer needs:
Public life, objectivity
Jukebox selection: *"Dream Weaver"*

Introducing Cancer

Cancerians are the zodiac's nurturers. Ruled by the Moon ☾, people born under the sign of the Crab have the ability to unlock others' deepest emotions. Friends, family, and strangers instinctively feel that it's safe to confide everything—from their most artistic dreams to their most selfish motives—in the presence of a Cancer. Being able to deeply connect with others has a dark side for Cancers, however. People born under this sign are often unable to channel their own messy emotions, feelings that can be difficult for them to control. Driven by a need for security, Cancerians are cautious about relationships. While many people rely on the Cancer in their life for emotional support, Crabs surround themselves with a small community, choosing to maintain links only with intimates they trust.

Crab children pamper their toys and pets and display remarkable empathy for others at a young age. During the teen years, Cancerian romanticism catapults boys and girls into steady dating. Their volatile emotions may propel them into early promiscuity or talk of marriage at a young age, but only if this will truly bring security. As adults, Cancerians remain close to their parents as well as their children, and relish the comings and goings of guests in their homes. While a career is important to them because they want the security that only money can buy, home and family takes first priority. Crabs may opt not to relocate for work if it means leaving the state where their extended family lives and instead try to get a promotion in their local office.

In their free time, Cancers relish playing with children, cooking, and decorating their homes. They are nesters, so any at-home activity suits them. The Cancerian ability to tap the unconscious often means these folks express themselves creatively through dance, art, music, or poetry. Because they connect exceptionally well with children, family reunions are always memorable for kids who spend time with a Cancer aunt or uncle. Life, for a Cancer, is about building and protecting close relationships.

Dedicated to Cancer

Crabs groove to sentimental tunes that stir their tender emotions. They seek songs that evoke bittersweet memories or inspire dreamy, creative moods.

Joyful — Cancerians have an infectious enthusiasm for life when they feel secure. *How Sweet It Is (To Be Loved by You)* sung by Marvin Gaye describes the euphoria they feel when all is harmonious.

Idealistic — Crabs look for the best in others and the world at large. *All I Have to Do Is Dream* performed by The Everly Brothers celebrates the quest for a sensitive world.

Domestic — *Endless Harmony* by The Beach Boys commemorates the energy of the Cancerian home, where Crabs nurture their long-lasting and passionate partnerships.

Emotional — Ruled by the moon, Crabs feel at liberty to express their feelings, a trait that *Mother Freedom* by Bread describes.

Romantic — *This Magic Moment* sung by The Drifters is an ode to Crabs' sentimental nature. This sign always remembers the tiny gestures, words, settings, and moments they share with loved ones.

Protective	Crabs carefully guard friends and lovers from harm. *Loves Me Like a Rock* as performed by The Dixie Hummingbirds pays tribute to this sign's protective approach.
Patriotic	As defenders of home and hearth, Crabs take pride in their nation. *This Is My Country* sung by The Impressions remembers this sign's belief in family and community.
Loving	Prone to falling in love, the sentimental Cancer wants to let everyone know, as in *Look at Me (I'm in Love)* performed by Moments.
Determined	*A Dream Goes on Forever* by Todd Rundgren applauds the spiritual strength that allows Crabs to commit to long-term goals.
Compassionate	*Kindness* by David Wilcox could be the theme song for Cancers, as empathy is one of this sign's most common traits.
Spiritual	Cancerians believe in following their dreams and can even motivate others to listen to their inner voices. *Dream Weaver* by Gary Wright celebrates this sign's mystical side.
Nurturing	From loving and kind to possessive and private, the archetypes of the Cancer persona are mythologized in *Cancer* by Canonball Adderley.

Cancer at Work

While their sensitive nature suggests that they're not well suited to the demands of a competitive job, innate intuition gives Cancerians good market timing that helps them excel in fields like investment banking or new product development. Cancerians befriend their colleagues and provide major social glue in any workplace, remembering special occasions and introducing rituals like Monday morning doughnuts that create social bonds between people. The need to produce riches, yet remain close to family, means Crabs will consider joining or running a small or family business. While blending the personal world with the professional world produces hazards for many signs, Cancerians can navigate the touchy successions and management situations a family company harbors. Crab managers can sense what motivates individual employees and assess which job roles might fulfill them—a talent that helps them retain staff. Their zany humor makes them fun colleagues.

Cancer Careers

Cancerian creativity is an asset in the workplace. Cancers not only know how to innovate, but they also know how to make products and services take on a friendly, family appeal. Cancerian Steve Wozniak co-founded Apple Computer, a company that made computers easy to use—especially at home. Meanwhile, Richard Branson, who runs Virgin Airlines, extended the company into new lines of business, including retail stores and Virgin's own brand of cola. While Cancers like to stay close to home, they're willing to go far in business to secure retirement. In business, Crabs can always call on their network of fiercely loyal contacts before putting a deal through. Because Cancers nurture others, a teaching career is a good bet. They also succeed in family medicine and as advocates for family causes: Faye Wattleton, Planned Parenthood's founder, is a Cancer, as are well-known doctors William Mayo and Alfred Kinsey. Domestically inclined, they make excellent decorators or renovators. They're also happy to dispense advice. Cancerian twins Abigail Van Buren and Ann Landers made careers out of responding to readers' requests for help.

Cancer in Love

Private Cancerians value domesticity and security in a relationship. They want to mother and be mothered by their mates. Men and women born under this sign crave partnership and warm up quickly when they feel a new acquaintance has relationship potential. Yet Crabs may sometimes shock significant others by pulling an abrupt about-face and ending a relationship over some subtle slight, which sensitive Cancer interprets as a sign that the relationship is doomed. Men of this sign make picky bachelors, because they want a woman who will both respect and mother them. Women may attract immature suitors before encountering the protective, down-to-earth mate that works best for them. Once they find their soulmates, Cancerians make wonderful partners—their offbeat humor, near-psychic ability to read others' feelings, and penchant for homemaking make them great companions. They need time alone to sort out their feelings, so a patient but strong-willed partner who can keep them in high spirits is a good match. They make loving parents and will want to nurture their mates as well as the children they'll have together.

Cancer Relationships

Cancer & Aries (*March 21 to April 20*)   Challenging

Cancer & Taurus (*April 21 to May 21*)   Passionate

Cancer & Gemini (*May 22 to June 21*)   Harmonious

Cancer & Cancer (*June 22 to July 22*)   Harmonious

Cancer & Leo (*July 23 to August 23*)   Harmonious

Cancer & Virgo (*August 24 to September 22*)   Passionate

Cancer & Libra (*September 23 to October 23*)   Challenging

Cancer & Scorpio (*October 24 to November 22*)   Passionate

Cancer & Sagittarius (*November 23 to December 21*) Challenging

Cancer & Capricorn (*December 22 to January 20*)   Passionate

Cancer & Aquarius (*January 21 to February 20*)   Challenging

Cancer & Pisces (*February 21 to March 20*)   Passionate

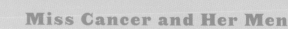

Men can't help falling for the fragile image projected by
Cancerian women like Liv Tyler or Meryl Streep.
Even tougher-seeming Crab women, like
Pamela Anderson, often appear to need special care.
That's just one side of Miss Cancer, though.
These women are strong and loyal, and will defend friends,
loved ones, and their own needs. They may
prefer a man who's a trustworthy provider and caretaker,
but he'll have to make it known
he respects her for letting him have the job.

Cancer Woman & Aries Man

Debbie Harry seeks Steven Tyler.

The mother of the zodiac likes Mr. Aries' enthusiastic boyishness. He's straightforward about what he wants—her—and he doesn't beat around the bush when it comes to declaring his intentions. These two operate on gut instincts, which can be both a blessing and a curse. Tactless Mr. Aries hurts Miss Cancer's feelings without even knowing it, and she sullenly retreats into her emotional shell. He hates it when she gets quiet; in fact, he'd prefer it if she yelled at him so he could defend himself. If she can learn to articulate her feelings before retreating, Mr. Aries will surprise her with an apology. In fact, she's one of the few women who can get past his pride and elicit one. Together they'll inspire shouting and tears in one another, but their passionate kiss-and-make-up scenes will compensate for the drama. He provides the fire and she provides the patience in this relationship, and this yin-yang energy will keep the home fires burning.

Cancer Woman & Taurus Man

Martha Reeves seeks Duke Ellington.

When this pair meets, they're so overwhelmed by their sexual attraction they may forget to stop and befriend one another first. It's atypical behavior for these two cautious characters, but when they've recovered from their passion they'll both be delighted to learn that they're as well suited to a life of domesticity together as they are a life of passion. These two homebodies will spend sentimental evenings pouring over photo albums, entertaining friends over dinner, and restoring their home. He'll listen to her colorful explanations of her emotional daily encounters, and she'll coax this reticent man into discussing his feelings. Miss Cancer approves of his love of routine, work ethic, and conservative investing strategies, and he won't mind her sentimentality. They'll finish each other's sentences and raise happy kids together. These two can keep the passion burning for decades.

Cancer Woman & Gemini Man

Nicolette Larson seeks Barry Manilow.

Like Peter Pan, the Gemini man flutters from one idea to the next. Miss Cancer likes the way he delights in the details other men overlook. When he recites poetry to her, invites her to curl up with the newspaper crossword puzzle, or insists she take a long lunch hour so they can share a picnic in the middle of a bustling park, she'll enjoy the way he knows how to find the serendipity in life. However, his shifting interests are a metaphor for his shifting fortunes: One week he's on the path to wealth and security, the next he's unemployed and loving it. It's fine to be creative, but Miss Cancer wants a man who can provide. She can't revel in the present if she's uncertain about the future. Mr. Gemini will sense he needs to take more responsibility with her than he has with other women. He'll also sense that, sexually, she needs a lover who is a bit more focused than he is—and less experimental. If he can live up to her high standards and provide the security she needs, Miss Cancer will support and even indulge the intellectual escapades he covets.

Cancer Woman & Cancer Man

Christine McVie seeks Mick Fleetwood.

Miss Cancer loves the way this sensitive man genuinely listens to her and is empathetic to others' feelings. Mr. Cancer is looking for someone to mother and understand him, and the Crab woman fits the bill. Even on a first date, these two will communicate on a deep, unconscious level and feel like old friends in a matter of hours. They'll cry together at movies and dream the same dreams. This pair of domestic nesters shares the same idea of nirvana: spending an evening in the kitchen with a neighbor, or sipping a cup of coffee after dinner and talking about the kids. They also share the same ethic about money—they need a lot, and they don't want to waste it. While they can have ugly fights when they're both in needy moods, they always recover and choose to make an even deeper commitment to one another. In bed, he is sweet and she is shy. In the world at large, they support one another every step of the way.

Cancer Woman & Leo Man

Linda Ronstadt seeks Kenny Rogers.

These two are like night and day: The Moon masks and changes her emotions constantly, while the Sun radiates nonstop charisma. While they both depend heavily on getting love and reassurance from a close romantic relationship, she needs commitment from just a small group of intimates while he needs attention from every passerby. He'll drag shy Miss Cancer right into the limelight with him, taking her away from her small, intensely intimate group. She'll beg her Leonine lover to stay home instead, and suggest they invite their friends over. Although she couldn't ask for a more demonstrative partner, she wishes he weren't so public about it. She likes to confine their sexual attraction to the bedroom, where she can be quite demonstrative herself. If they can balance their public and private lives, this macho guy and this feminine lady will live happily ever after.

Cancer Woman & Virgo Man

Carly Simon seeks Van Morrison.

This shy pair recognize in one another the healing qualities that make them both popular with their friends. She views Mr. Virgo as a saint in a world full of werewolves—the kind of guy who would return a lost wallet to its original owner without stealing a penny. Meanwhile, sweet-natured Miss Cancer is so friendly that he manages to overcome his inhibitions and ask her out. Throughout their relationship, he provides practical advice and genuinely likes helping people, and she provides a shoulder to cry on in times of trouble. In one another, they each find a sane partner who can appreciate those subtle personality traits that other, more extroverted lovers overlooked in them. Mr. Virgo is a surprisingly passionate lover and Miss Cancer is often surprisingly more experienced in private than she appears at first. Their relationship will grow better and better over time.

Cancer Woman & Libra Man

Emily Saliers seeks Tom Petty.

Though sociable Mr. Libra may not seem like a good fit for private Miss Cancer, he depends on partnership as much as she does. The two of them need different things in a mate, however: She needs someone who understands her feelings, while he needs someone who listens to his ideas. They also have different ideas of what makes for a good time—he wants to go places with a mate by his side, while she wants to end the party-hopping life she so abhorred when she was single. However, they can take turns indulging one another. Miss Cancer doesn't mind going places when she has a trusted companion at her side. Since these two love enjoying a well-kept home, Mr. Libra can always bring the party home, or entertain guests while Miss Cancer spends time in her quiet corner of the garden. They rarely fight, but he has a way of intellectualizing his feelings that confuses Miss Cancer, and her silences baffle this diplomatic man. However, because both signs value relationships, these two can build a good partnership together if they iron out their differences and accent the positive.

Cancer Woman & Scorpio Man

Li'l Kim seeks Puff Daddy.

His dark side inspires Miss Cancer, who empathizes with him. Her sensitivity disarms Mr. Scorpio, who drops his tough-guy act to gallantly protect her. They are both needy—and want a partner to respond to their changing emotions—but their ability to nurture one another is instinctual. He'll sense when Miss Cancer needs time alone and quietly slip out of the room, and she'll sidle up next to him on the couch while he tells her about his difficult day. In bed, they create romantic scenes straight out of the movies. Because Mr. Scorpio easily explains his feelings—and intuits hers—their fights are infrequent. He's money-minded and ambitious, so together they can build a lifestyle she enjoys. He likes romance as much as she does, so he'll remember to celebrate little holidays like the day they met or the first time they kissed. She'll leave little love notes in his briefcase, and he'll surprise her by coming home early so they can watch the old movies that makes them both cry. It's a natural, easygoing relationship that could certainly lead to marriage.

Cancer Woman & Sagittarius Man

Cyndi Lauper seeks Ted Nugent.

♂ ♀

She'll demand that this creative philosopher mature if he wants to capture her romantic, but decidedly grown-up, heart. Mr. Sagittarius finds this fragile woman easy to talk to, and he appreciates the way she asks questions and genuinely listens to him. She'd never leave home for more than a week—not without bringing her photo album or her grandmother's good-luck quilt. Yet despite the wanderlust tugging at his heart, he may decide to give life with her a try. After all, this sexy woman knows all sorts of ways to keep them entertained should he choose to stay home. It won't always be easy for either of them, for this traveling man has trouble settling down, while this domestic woman has trouble traveling. However, if Miss Cancer allows herself to let romance override her pragmatism and let him lead her to new places, she could learn to be at home in the world as well as in her den. If Mr. Sagittarius decides to let himself be tamed a little bit, he'll realize that rather than move all over the place looking for the next new experience he could experience true love right by Miss Cancer's side.

Cancer Woman & Capricorn Man

Kim Carnes seeks Rod Stewart.

A romantic man lives beneath his pin-striped exterior, but sometimes Miss Cancer has a hard time finding him. Though Mr. Capricorn is chivalrous at first, it's a role that doesn't always come naturally for him. He's sensitive like she is, but has a hard time showing it. The two of them do share big financial ambitions, but she may wish he would spend more time at home nurturing her and less time at the office. He will find her silences hard to read, yet she has a way of arousing feelings he's never had for another woman. They both want a serious commitment or none at all and both will discuss, at an early stage, their hopes for a long-term union. As long as he remembers to provide romantic surprises and remind her he cares, and as long as she realizes he shows he cares by working to build the secure future they both want, these two could have a very successful relationship. In bed, he is demonstrative and she is nurturing. If emotionally savvy Miss Cancer puts her faith in him, she'll realize this quiet guy has a heart of gold that only gets more valuable as time passes.

Cancer Woman & Aquarius Man

Courtney Love seeks Kurt Cobain.

She finds this wacky independent man relaxing. He's commitment-shy, but they share common values: Both are intensely loyal to friends and like to be there for other people. The problem here is that Mr. Aquarius has a looser definition of friendship than Miss Cancer does. He'll invite home any stray from a bar or political rally, he'll open his doors and coffers to numerous causes, and he never hoards money like his Crab lady does. Mr. Aquarius reasons that you can't take it with you and spends easily, invoking the spirit of brotherly love. However, if they keep separate bank accounts so she knows where the rainy-day backup is—and just how much of it there is—she can get beyond this hurdle in their relationship. Since detached Mr. Aquarius feels like an old friend to her rather than a regular suitor, their sex life may lack the drama she's had with other partners, but can, with effort, be satisfying. Though they may have to work to keep the relationship lively for him and secure for her, their empathy toward each other makes them a happy couple.

Cancer Woman & Pisces Man

Lena Horne seeks Roger Daltrey.

Sometimes Miss Cancer finds that "sensitive" men are all talk and no sincerity, but that isn't the case with emotional Mr. Pisces. He delivers on both fronts—not to mention in bed, where their evenings together are poetic. He doesn't like to rest in one place for long, but with gentle Miss Cancer in his life he rethinks this tendency. When women get frustrated at his occasional lack of focus, he grows sensitive and morose, but this empathetic lady understands rather than criticizes the way his mind and emotions work. In fact, maybe for the first time in his life, he wants to be right where he is. In this relationship, these two will try to guard against their selfish tendency toward sulking. Each will strive to become the available, strong person the other needs in a partner. Though they are both very emotional, which makes for lively conversations and the occasional fight with tears, this relationship will remain uncomplicated. These two will fall in love at first sight and will never take their eyes off each other over the years.

Mr. Cancer and His Women

Sensitive New Age guys Tom Hanks and
Harrison Ford are both nurturing Cancerians. However,
Crab guys can also be macho and tough, like
Sylvester Stallone and Tom Cruise. Some Cancer men
fear no woman can truly understand their sensitivity.
Since this sign is monogamy-oriented,
though, they will pursue intimate relationships.
The Cancer man quietly encourages
his mate to express her feelings and reminds her that,
no matter what, he loves her for who she is.

Cancer Man & Aries Woman

Huey Lewis seeks Loretta Lynn.

This sharp-tongued, bossy lady knows what she likes, and he feels lucky when she fixes her eye on him. She'll mistake the quiet Crab man for a passive, fun-loving person she can dominate, but will soon learn that if she wants to pursue him she won't necessarily end up in charge. Miss Aries and Mr. Cancer both run on impulse and gut instincts, only her instincts rouse her to action while his stir up complex emotions. She recovers far more quickly than he does from mistakes, scares, and hurts and goes through life with an enthusiasm he'd love to adopt. They communicate clearly as long as she curbs her tactlessness. When she hurts his feelings, he retreats into silence. Oddly enough, what bonds this unusual pair is their complementary senses of humor. He states what other people are feeling in the funniest way and has a knack for imitation, while her slapstick style makes him double over with the giggles. If they can keep the laughter alive in the living room—and bedroom—this relationship will benefit.

Cancer Man & Taurus Woman

Louis Armstrong seeks Ella Fitzgerald.

♀ ♂

This earth mother really knows how to shake up staid Mr. Cancer. Her va-va-voom curves and sensual voice make him as distracted as a teenager. Mr. Cancer and Miss Taurus value security, family, and routine, not to mention nurturing their friends. She enjoys taking care of their belongings, while he loves collecting stuff that reminds him of good times past. They both want to marry immediately, but go through with a long courtship just for appearances since they both respect tradition. In the meantime, she'll secretly study the decorating catalogs for the house she wants to own with him, and he'll read parenting books in anticipation of the kids he wants to father. Her great cooking skills and steady emotions buffer him against the world, while his poetic sensitivity and manly affections reassure her. This domestic pair is proof that staying at home doesn't have to be boring. Their sexual compatibility and comfort with one another only get better and better as time passes.

Cancer Man & Gemini Woman

Arlo Guthrie seeks Wynonna Judd.

When this cerebral, changeable man meets this sensitive, moody woman, anything goes. He could learn from her brainy detachment to better move through life's ups and downs unscathed. She could learn from his willingness to take care of the boring details she abhors—like paying the mortgage, getting the trees pruned, and remembering to tuck the juice boxes in their kids' school lunch bags. She may lose patience with his retiring moods and fail to understand why he's not as social as she is. He may dislike her lack of compassion and resent her scathing comments during the sentimental movies that make him weep. However, if she uses her diplomacy skills to help him voice his feelings and doesn't blow their nest egg on Cinco de Mayo party favors, Mr. Cancer can come to accept her airy detachment. Opposites attract—and, in this case, may stick together. If she learns to value domesticity and he learns to voice his pleasure, these two could make each day feel like a celebration.

Cancer Man & Cancer Woman

Marc Cohn seeks Suzanne Vega.

♀ ♂

The question isn't which of them will cry, it's which of these sensitive souls will cry first. Neither Mr. nor Miss Cancer has enough objectivity to see where the problems in this relationship will crop up—which is the problem itself, since the sensitivity that drew them together is also what will tug them apart at times. They both sulk when they're upset, and if they're upset simultaneously no one will come around to coax each of them out of their respective funks. If they commit to a life together—and with their physical attraction and love of nesting, there's no reason why they shouldn't—they'll each have to overcome the selfishness that they try to disguise from the rest of the world. Few outsiders imagine that passive Cancers are capable of withholding as much emotion as they share. Helping each other overcome this trait will be the key to unlocking their deeper intimacy.

Cancer Man & Leo Woman

Ruben Blades seeks Tori Amos.

He likes her positive attitude, generosity, and emotionally forthright approach. She needs as much attention as he does, and they shower one another with affection. However, she needs an audience both in her intimate relationships and in her larger life. If she takes her quest for the spotlight public—and drags retiring Mr. Cancer there in the process—he won't like it one bit. For this relationship to work, Miss Leo will need to find outside outlets for her drama. He can nurture her substantial ego and enjoy her kooky high-jinks, but he likes to retain his own privacy. They may also disagree about money. While he respects the impulse behind her generosity, he also wants them to have money to retire. If she realizes she doesn't have to buy her way into popularity or wear expensive head-turning fashions to keep him, this problem should disappear. Her enthusiastic show of affection in bed will make him feel completely adored. With compromise, these two make a good match for the long haul—as friends, lovers, and partners.

Cancer Man & Virgo Woman

Jeff Beck seeks LeAnn Rimes.

♀   ♂

Many men balk at Miss Virgo's criticisms, but Mr. Cancer recognizes her nit-picks as attempts to make him a better man. He also recognizes her as a person every bit as nurturing—and deserving of nurturing—as he is. Now and then her need for order and propriety will feel like overkill, and he'll snap when she corrects his grammar or manners. The hurt look on her face, though, will swiftly bring about an apology between them. These two adore each other, and don't like to pick fights for attention. Sometimes she'll have trouble addressing his silent moods. For the most part, however, there will be few tears and lots of laughter between these two. She understands his caution and domesticity, while he allows her to engage in her somewhat compulsive routines. Physically, his sweet embraces melt away her perfectionism and her affections remind him that when she falls, it's serious. Marriage seems like a likely bet for these two.

Cancer Man & Libra Woman

Woody Guthrie seeks Tanya Tucker.

She seems a bit lost, but he's willing to offer her a helping hand. Her confusion, though, appears to be permanent, for Miss Libra lives in a world of conflicting ideas. Moody Mr. Cancer doesn't get much grounding from this airy woman, who changes her hair color as often as she changes her mind. Yet because they both cherish monogamy, and she wants to talk things through, they'll try and find a middle ground. Sometimes she doesn't speak her mind because she doesn't want to hurt others, and he'll break her of this habit by teaching her to be forthright. Sometimes he has trouble articulating how he feels, and she'll help him better communicate his feelings. Both Mr. Cancer and Miss Libra love the trappings of romance. She likes to hear sweet talk, and he feels at home with poetry. Sexually, she's a little ethereal for him—he doesn't always know if she's having a good time—but here, as in other parts of the relationship, they can come to a kind of compromise. Outsiders will never know what they're thinking, but will sense that Mr. Cancer and Miss Libra are well suited to sharing domestic life together.

Cancer Man & Scorpio Woman

Carlos Santana seeks Grace Slick.

The Crab man likes Miss Scorpio's rough edges and dark secrets. Physically, their attraction is intense. At times he's too thin-skinned for her liking, but she respects him for his emotional depth. Few men offer more compassion toward this woman than Mr. Cancer. She's been around the block, come back for more, and gone around again. She may not look tired on the outside, but she's packed so much pain, love, sex, mystery, and excitement into her life that she's very nearly bursting at the seams from the drama of it all. Unlike other men she's been with who have a hard time with her strength and experience, Mr. Cancer doesn't judge her—and she has the depth to know the value of this. They will build a private nest together and share a comfortable home.

Cancer Man & Sagittarius Woman

Kris Kristofferson seeks Sinead O'Connor.

As the zodiac's true wanderer, Miss Sagittarius realizes that this homebody of a man needs someone experienced in his life. She has seen and done things he's only considered, and although Miss Sagittarius never stops moving for long, she'll slow down to listen to Mr. Cancer's probing questions. It won't take him long to figure out that she remains on the go because she hasn't found the sort of true love that might keep her in one place. Moving in with him may be the beginning of her most educational journey. He'll teach her that adventure doesn't always involve travel, and that they can learn more by exploring their emotions and affections in private together than she could had she stayed alone on the open road. She'll teach him that sometimes you have to leave home to appreciate it. Sexually, she's a bit intense for him—but as they grow familiar with one another he'll happily experiment to provide the spice she requires. Together, they can build a solid bridge between their two different worlds. It won't be an easy bridge, but when complete it will be beautiful and not at all what either of them expected.

Cancer Man & Capricorn Woman

George Michael seeks Sade.

In this relationship, sensitive Mr. Cancer stirs up buttoned-up Miss Capricorn's hidden sentimentality. She will try and resist her fluttering heart by bossing him around, and he may sulk when the woman he knows is so sensitive tries to hide her true desires from him. In the end, though, they'll end up in bed, where he has the sweetest way of convincing her no harm will come if she loosens up and enjoys letting love into her life. As long as she remains receptive to the intense feelings this empathetic man elicits from her, Mr. Cancer will enjoy spending time in this relationship. They share a strong desire for material security, a warm home, and family. She'll get him to laugh at his oversensitivity, and he'll get her to laugh at her workaholic need for control. They make an odd, but oddly solid, couple. Marriage is inevitable—as are many years of good times.

Cancer Man & Aquarius Woman

Ringo Starr seeks Sheryl Crow.

He likes unconventional people, and in Miss Aquarius, he finds society's original contrarian. He supports her altruism and need to participate in social causes. However, if he wants to have her all to himself he'll have to teach her that an intimate relationship is as important as the causes she hopes will improve their community. Miss Aquarius considers the world her family and sees no need to marry and settle down. Mr. Cancer can teach her, though, that she's a better humanitarian when she has a steady, intimate life to come home to at the end of the day. If she lets him take care of the finances—which she might handle carelessly—and appreciates that having a home base makes her a better world citizen, these two could enjoy a friendly relationship that could lead to more. Sexually, she's more experimental than he is, but over time he'll adapt surprisingly well to her style. This empathetic couple will live in tune with the times and participate in charitable causes.

Cancer Man & Pisces Woman

Gustav Mahler seeks Tracy Chapman.

Mr. Cancer provides a steady shoulder for her to cry on. She feels she can tell him all her tales of woe, problems brought on by her misguided optimism. He's touched by her idealism, and she's touched that he doesn't find her a gullible fool. Both of them need to feel needed, and each knows how to make the other feel secure. Sexually, they share evenings of utterly poetic bliss. Mr. Cancer loves helping Miss Pisces overcome her negative mood swings. Because she's an idealist who chooses to sympathize and see only the best in people and situations, her compassion for others often borders on denial. When she slips on her rose-colored glasses, life looks better to her, yet she secretly knows she's avoiding the full picture. Mr. Cancer is touched by her goodness, but can also help her face reality head on. With a trusty mate like him in her life, she can tackle the world's woes without losing her unique outlook. After all, if her emotions overwhelm her, she can always lean on him for support. This sentimental pair will enjoy a spiritual, unconditional love.

Cancer at Home

The Cancer home is a gated sanctuary, a restful, cozy space hidden away from the rest of the world. Crabs are collectors, and their rooms overflow with objects chosen not so much for style as for sentimental value. A Cancer will tack up a grandchild's finger painting next to a priceless watercolor that's been passed down through the family for five generations. Because meal planning and preparation are favorite Cancerian activities, these folks will have a state-of-the-art kitchen equipped with top-quality gadgets and pantries filled with all the right spices. Every Cancer needs a quiet private place to reflect. This sign relaxes around water, so a large bathroom with an old-fashioned tub, a bench by a backyard goldfish pond, or access to a nearby lake can provide a place for meditation. Sentimental Crabs will hesitate to convert their grown kids' rooms into offices or spare guest rooms, as they secretly cling to the idea that they'll come home again.

Cancer Health

The Cancerian body can be slim and narrow or rounded and maternal. Cancer rules the breasts, chest, and stomach, which means that people born under this sign are susceptible to stomach upset as well as colds that develop into bronchitis. As Cancer is a water sign, they retain water weight easily and will need to moderate their use of salt and alcohol. They keep extra cardigans and changes of shoes on hand at home and at work, since their response to changes in temperature will otherwise distract them. They are also susceptible to diabetes, so they need to watch the sweet tooth. Because Crabs are sensitive, regular practice of meditation, yoga, or tai chi can help moderate their emotions. Sports that bring them near the water, such as swimming, sailing, fishing, or canoeing, are also beneficial for this water sign. More sensitive to touch than people born under most other signs, Cancers enjoy foot and back massages as well as long soaks in the bathtub.

Cancer Style

Cancers wear tailored clothes that are slightly loose-fitting, as if to simultaneously convey that they are flexible people who also take a practical approach to life. They're most often seen wearing a pale shade of blue—frequently in a metallic or grayish shade. Oscar de la Renta, Pierre Cardin, Bill Blass, and Giorgio Armani are all Cancerian designers, stylists who create clothes in the subtle style Crab natives favor. Cancers are conservative shoppers, but are picky about clothes because their outfits express their moods. That's why they opt for separates that blend easily, or multiple pieces from one designer's line that work together interchangeably. Cancer's special stone is the moonstone—though Cancer kids may like to wear mood rings. This sign loves fine bath and shaving products, and Cancerians will opt to use high-quality body lotions on their sensitive skin. Crabs of both sexes like fresh, citrus-smelling aftershaves and perfumes that remind them of the beach and summertime.

On the Road with Cancer

When Cancers go on vacation, they want lots of friends and family around and they like to create a homey environment wherever they go. This means they'll want to rent a house, cabin, or apartment so the family can all stay nearby. They favor water-related vacations where they can unwind, so the Bahamas, Bermuda, or Key West (where Cancerian Ernest Hemingway lived) appeal to them. They don't like to venture too far from home, and, since they love planning trips that are fun for the kids, don't mind renting a cabin or setting up camp at a nearby state park or touring state capitals. As the zodiac's patriots, Cancers also like to see historic sites—canyons, monuments, museums, and restored colonial towns.

Cancer Entertaining

Cancerians prefer making comfort foods to crafting trendy cuisine. They love family events and will readily volunteer to host family reunions, anniversary and retirement parties, or graduation ceremonies. Every Cancer has an old recipe file of family favorites that have been passed on from generation to generation, and they see re-creating dishes from the past as a way of preserving family. They like to churn homemade ice cream, pull out a jar of homemade butter pickles, or serve grandma's meatballs on pasta. While they dish the entrée, they'll tell stories about the recipes. To Cancerians, any event is a family event—come one, come all. They'll be happy if everyone has eaten their fill and learned something new about each other in the process, especially if the event allows them to take more pictures for their overstuffed photo albums.

In the Company of Cancer

Musicians:
Louis Armstrong
Jeff Beck
Rubén Blades
Laura Branigan
Kim Carnes
Marc Cohn
Mick Fleetwood
  (Fleetwood Mac)
Nanci Griffith
Arlo Guthrie
Woody Guthrie
Debbie Harry (Blondie)
Lena Horne
Li'l Kim
Kris Kristofferson
Nicolette Larson
Cyndi Lauper
Huey Lewis
Courtney Love (Hole)
Gustav Mahler
Christine McVie
  (Fleetwood Mac)
George Michael
Della Reese
Martha Reeves
Linda Ronstadt
Emily Saliers
  (Indigo Girls)
Carlos Santana
Carly Simon

Ringo Starr
Suzanne Vega

Performers:
Dan Aykroyd
Kevin Bacon
Kathy Bates
Milton Berle
Sandra Bullock
Mel Brooks
Phoebe Cates
Bill Cosby
Tom Cruise
John Cusack
Willem Dafoe
Carson Daly
Brian Dennehy
Shelley Duvall
Harrison Ford
Fred Grandy
Merv Griffin
Tom Hanks
Lena Horne
Cheryl Ladd
Pamela Anderson
John Lovitz
Slim Pickens
Gilda Radner
Ginger Rogers
Richard Simmons
Sylvester Stallone
Meryl Streep

Liv Tyler
Lindsay Wagner
Robin Williams
Natalie Wood

Reformers:
John Calvin
Dalai Lama
Emma Goldman
Helen Keller
Alfred Kinsey
Marshall McLuhan
Georges Pompidou
Lady Diana Spencer
Jesse Ventura
Faye Wattleton

Artists:
Marc Chagall
Corneille
Edgar Degas
Bob Fosse
Oscar Hammerstein
Edward Hopper
Frida Kahlo
Gustav Klimt
Rembrandt
Twyla Tharp
James B. Wyeth

Athletes:
Arthur Ashe
John Elway

"Shoeless Joe" Jackson
Greg LeMond
Carl Lewis
Satchel Paige
Richard Petty

Writers:
Richard Bach
Saul Bellow
Ambrose Bierce
Pearl S. Buck
Louise Erdrich
Natalia Ginzburg
Nathaniel Hawthorne
Mark Helprin
Ernest Hemingway
Hermann Hesse
Franz Kafka
Dean Koontz
Alice McDermott
Pablo Neruda
George Orwell
Luigi Pirandello
Marcel Proust
Antoine de Saint-Exupéry
George Sand
Neil Simon
Isaac Bashevis Singer
Jean Stafford
Tom Stoppard
Hunter S. Thompson
E. B. White